ARTISTS' CHRISTMAS CARDS

COMPILED BY STEVEN HELLER

F A FIRESIDE BOOK
Published by Simon and Schuster
NEW YORK

Copyright © 1979 by Steven Heller

First Fireside Edition, 1981
Published by Simon and Schuster
A Division of Gulf & Western Corporation
Simon & Schuster Building
Rockefeller Center
1230 Avenue of the Americas
New York, New York 10020

Published by arrangement with A&W Publishers, Inc.

FIRESIDE and colophon are trademarks of Simon & Schuster

Manufactured in the United States of America

1 2 3 4 5 6 7 8 9 10 Pbk.

Library of Congress Cataloging in Publication Data

Main entry under title:
Artists' Christmas cards.
  (A Fireside book)
  Reprint. Originally published: New York:
A & W Publishers, 1979.
    1. Christmas cards.   2. Artists—Psychology.
I. Heller, Steven.
NC1866.C5A77   1981   741.68'4   81-9084
ISBN 0-671-43773-9 Pbk.   AACR2

ACKNOWLEDGEMENTS

HIS page is devoted to the many friends and acquaintances who have helped with the preparation of this book.

Sarah Jane Freymann who, because of her support, energy and love, made this book a reality. Brad Holland for his invaluable enthusiasm and friendship. Fritz Eichenberg, whose personal collection of Christmas cards was an important beginning for me. Edward Gorey, probably unbeknownst to himself, for a phone call at just the right moment. Sel Lederman, whose words at a difficult time will be treasured. Angela Miller, a wonderful editor, who made this book happen.

Many people were kind enough to open their cartons and files and make available approximately 4000 cards for me to see—without them there would be no book. Ted Riley and John Locke, two of the most intelligent and caring art agents I have known, represent a number of the artists whose works are shown in this book. The following galleries and their directors either loaned me cards or suggested their artists contact me: thanks to Grace Borgenicht, Borgenicht Gallery; Sylvan Cole, Associated American Artists; Monique Knowlton, Knowlton Gallery; Nancy Hoffman, Hoffman Gallery; David Kermani, Tibor Di Nagy Gallery; Alladar Marhburger, Fischbach Gallery; Kathy Markell, Markell Gallery; Marty and Joan Sumers, Sumers Gallery; Andy Fitch, Fitch-Febrel Gallery; Terry Dittenfass, Dittenfass Gallery; Jack Alonzo, Alonzo Gallery and the Nobe Gallery. Thanks also to the artists who allowed me to ravage their personal collections: Arnold Roth, John Baeder, Diana Bryan, Lee Naiman, Robert Andrew Parker, Carol Wald, Jack Ziegler, Harvey Kurtzman and Art Spiegelman.

Kneeland McNulty, curator of prints at the Philadelphia Museum of Art, was kind enough to guide me through the scores of cards in the Zigrosser Collection, probably the largest and most enjoyable collection I've seen. Joan Davidson of Artists' Postcards generously exchanged artists with me. Anne Elizabeth Suter of Diogenese Verlag, Zurich, supplied me with lovely cards and extraordinary assistance. And Bernie Reilly, curator of Applied Graphic Arts at the Library of Congress, has consistently been of service with all my research projects.

I am also indebted to the following people who have helped, aided and abetted in the compilation and design of this volume: Al Hawkins, Elliott Banfield, Paul Degen, Steven Guarnaccia, Bill Lee, Arnie Levin, Steve Schwartz, Gary Hoenig, George Woods, Julia Batchelder, Andy Kner, Leslie Cabarga, Ruth Ansel, Harvey Shapiro, Mike Valenti, Lou Silverstein, Diane Villani, Cecile Bazelon, Philippe Weisbecker, Toni Eichenberg, Paul Davis, Ed Spiro, Marshall Arisman, Jasmine Katz, Ralph Steadman, Maurice Sendak, Frans de Boer, Eugene Mihaesco and all of those whose cards could not appear in this volume.

And most of all, to my wife, Julia Goggin, who has been a big support and has put up graciously with boxes and portfolios of Christmas cards all over the house for over a year.

INTRODUCTION

THE ornaments, carols and traditions of Christmas are very special to me. I have always loved the holiday season.

As a child, I waited impatiently for the mailman to deliver the first Christmas card. It usually arrived shortly after Thanksgiving and others followed each day after that—the mailbox would be stuffed with colorful greetings that I hung all over the house. I took it as something of a personal challenge to cover every inch of spare wall space, and when I was lucky enough to receive an idealized snow scene of New York City (my favorite kind of card), I carefully displayed it in a prominent place.

Every year the cards stayed up until New Year's Day, when I would store them away in a closet. I saved them. I saved almost all of them for years; I guess it was my ongoing connection with the holiday (or a collector's neurosis).

Christmas is still special for me. It is also special for the illustrators, printmakers, cartoonists, painters and sculptors whose cards are collected in this book. Some of the cards are one-of-a-kind works of art sent as special gifts to close friends. Others are from limited print runs, while still others were produced especially for this book and for use as this year's card. None, however, were designed for mass commercial use.

Ever since I began collecting the personal cards sent to me, I was fascinated by how different artists interpreted the symbols of the season. Many reworked familiar visual clichés to create unique and personal images. As you will see, the cards in this collection are varied in technique, attitude and subject matter. They range from the beautiful to the grotesque; from the loving to the cynical. But above all, they are *statements* that reflect their creators.

Not every one represented here loves Christmas, but all have something original to say about it. This originality was my criterion in making selections for this book. Actually, I first set out to assemble a collection of cards from well-known *masters,* both vintage and modern. I found, however, that by and large their season's greetings were not Christmassy at all, but simply reproductions (and some originals) of their current work. They were beautiful in their own right, but did not reflect any personal feeling for the holiday. Looking in a different direction, I found that cartoonists and illustrators, people who use symbolic language daily to communicate, created the most interesting, unique and humorous cards. To this group I added the works of painters, printmakers and writers who were moved by Christmas to create images that did *not* rely on any of the familiar clichés. I have, therefore, included the best and most original work I have seen, and I have seen well over 4000 cards.

Although I enjoy all of the pieces included here, I have a special appreciation for Brad Holland's *Santa Claus,* Ripley Albright's *Gifts,* Philippe Weisbecker's *Rooftops* and Don Nice's *Crayons*—to look at them is to smile.

I am happy to have found the vintage cards by Paul Cadmus, Harvey Kurtzman, Rockwell Kent and Alexander Calder, artists whom I greatly admire. The cards by Arnie Roth, R. O. Blechman, Gahan Wilson and Marshall Arisman are only a few examples of the annual treats these artists send, while the works by Ralph Cava, Ilse Getz, Randy Enos and Paul Degen are one of a kind created for this book.

As an art director, I work with visual images all the time, but it is only at Christmas that I get home delivery, only at Christmas that an artist communicates in precisely this way, only at Christmas that people can be so intimately connected. Each envelope yields a different message, and a different emotion. When the season ends I am already looking forward to the next year and the surprises that *it* will bring.

It is a pleasure to share this collection of cards with you. I hope that you are as pleased by looking at them now as I was when I saw them for the first time.

Steve Heller

THE ARTISTS

In Order of Appearance

Ed Koren	Henrik Drescher	Pierre Le Tan
Ralph Cava	Michael Sporn	Victor Juhasz
John Baeder	Devis Grebu	Gailard Sartain
André Francois	Don Nice	Elwood Smith
Rockwell Kent	Cliff Condak	Robert Osborn
Philippe Weisbecker	Harvey Kurtzman	Mark Podwal
David Itchkawitch	Arnold Levin	Sigeru Taniguchi
Guy Billout	Margery Caggiano	Joan Hall
Nicky Zann	Ray Ciarrochi	Ralph Steadman
Ripley Albright	Tony Auth	John Baeder
Elliott Banfield	Jeanne Grundberg	Tom Wolfe
Randy Enos	R. O. Blechman	Christin Couture
Paul Flora	Bobby London	Art Spiegelman
Ilse Getz	John Craig	Diana Bryan
Robert Cuneo	Tomi Ungerer	Michael Knigen
Alexander Walsh	Steven Guarnaccia	Edward Gorey
Patrick Flynn	Edward Sorel	Marshall Arisman

John Caldwell	Gail Geltner	Michael ffolkes
Robert Tallon	Hank Virgona	Wallace Wood
Gary Hallgren	Sara Midda	Cecile Bazelon
Phyllis Herfield	Ronald Searle	Tom Hachtman
Arnold Roth	Alexa Grace	Johnny Hart
Bill Charmatz	Gahan Wilson	Joseph Goldyne
Bill Woodman	Warrington Colescott	Paul Cadmus
Doug Taylor	Walter Stein	Frans de Boer (Efbe)
Jean-Pierre Descloseaux	Bill Lee	Edward Koren
David Itchkawitch	Carol Anthony	James Grashow
Carol Wald	Hans P. Schaad	Paul Flora
Marty Norman	Fritz Eichenberg	John H. Hawkins
Inez Storer	Walt Kelly	Steven Guarnaccia
Gahan Wilson	Jay Lynch	Marshall and Dee Arisman
Cathy Barancik	Jack Ziegler	Christopher Hewat
Allan Lewis	Tomi Ungerer	Gordon Kibbee
Paul Degen	Charles Addams	Leslie Cabarga
Randal Rupert	Maurice Sendak	George Constant
Tom Kleh	Günter Grass	Eugene Mihaesco
Arnold Roth	Brad Holland	Alexander Calder
	Edward Gorey	

ANDRE FRANCOIS

PHILIPPE WEISBECKER

ITCH 74

NICKY ZANN

The Simple Purveyor of Gifts

SINTER·CLAES

SEASONS GREETINGS FROM LEANN+RANDALL ENOS

ROBERT CUNEO

THE · WINTER · SOLSTICE · NAP

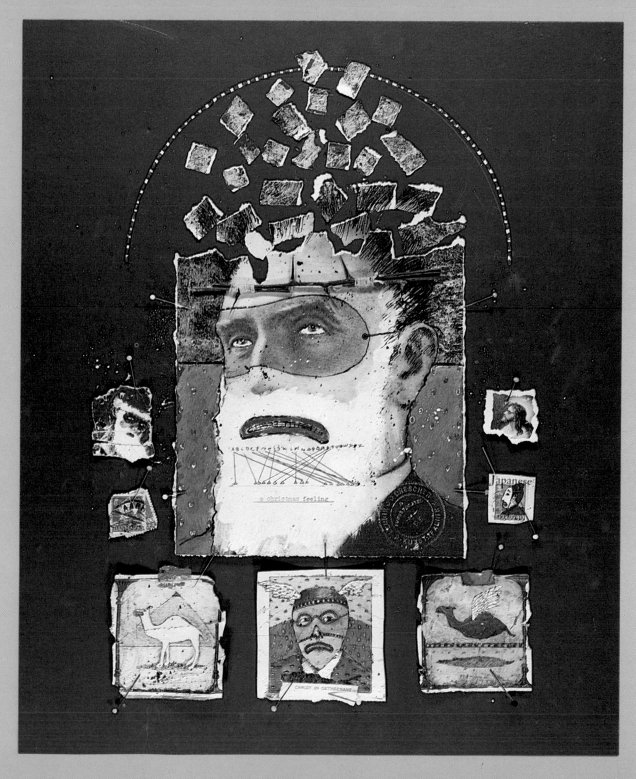

MICHAEL SPORN

merry christmas
cliff condak

Buckeye Studio, 15 N. Walnut St.,
CANTON, - OHIO.
Ground Floor.

MARGERY CAGGIANO

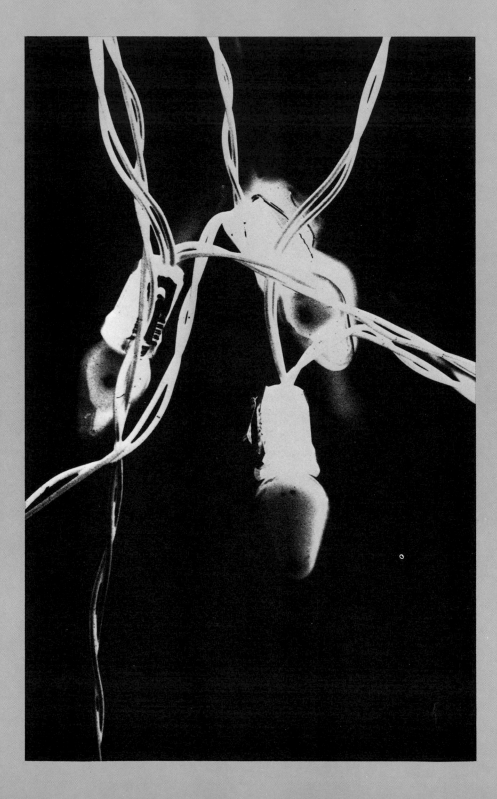

RAY CIARROCHI

MERRY CHRISTMAS 76

R.O. BLECHMAN

JOHN CRAIG

Remember the Greediest

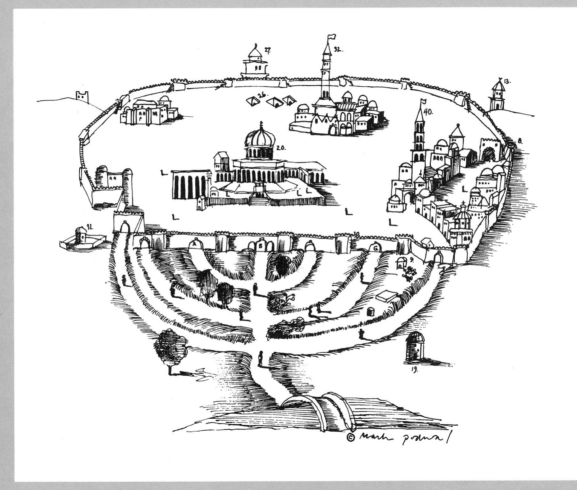

JOAN HALL

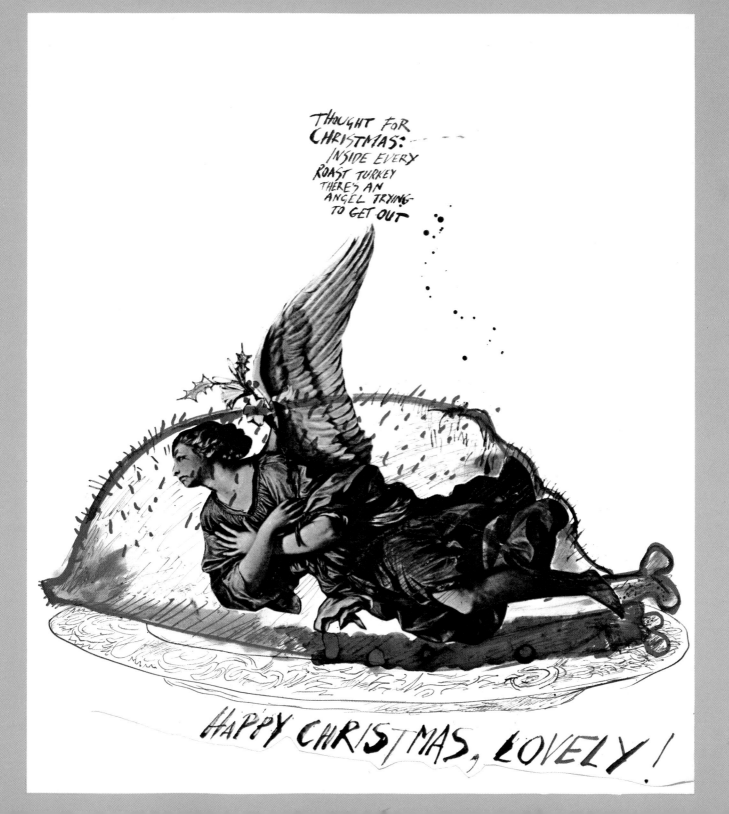

JOHN BAEDER

MERRY CHRISTMAS

noël

HAPPY
HOLIDAYS

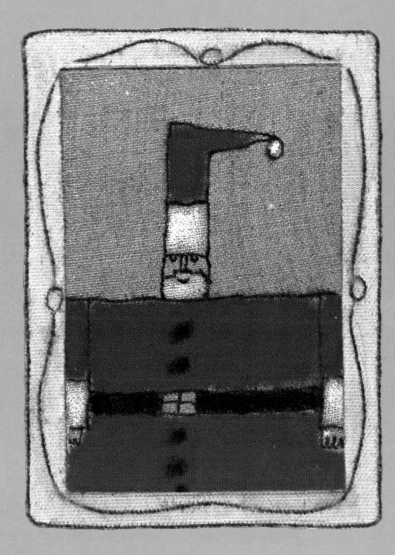

GARY HALLGREN

"Christmas in the Country"

PHYLLIS HERFIELD

Merry Christmas 1975

" DON'T BOTHER SANTA, HE HASN'T HAD
HIS COFFEE YET. "

JEAN-PIERRE DESCLOSEAUX

desclozeaux

DAVID ITCHKAWITCH

JUST A JOLLY GREETING

CATHY BARANCIK

PAUL DEGEN

RANDAL RUPERT

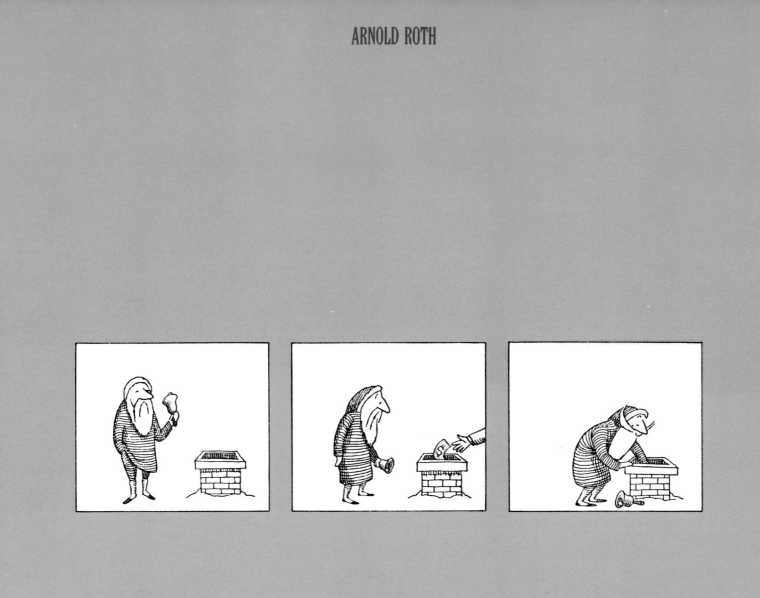

22/50   Merry Christmas,   Virgona 1977

SARA MIDDA

AT CHRISTMAS TIME WE HUNG OUR STOCKINGS ON THE GAS RANGE.

HANS P. SCHAAD

ISAIAH II ✡ FRITZ EICHENBERG 1976

Gertrude Stein as a child

decorates a dog for Christmas.

1976

STEVEN GUARNACCIA

THE CAT AND THE PENCIL
Conducted by Dee and Marshall Arisman December, 1972

That animals can display originality and inventiveness has been asserted since Aesop. For the last five Christmases, we have conducted our own scientific experiment dealing with an animal's ability to draw a recognizable object. This year we have made an important breakthrough. The following is an account of the experiment: Lanta, our 12 year old female, sealpoint siamese cat was locked in a box, 3' x 4', for a period of two weeks prior to Christmas Day. The box was equipped with a No. 2 lead pencil (with eraser), a 4 inch decorated artificial fir tree, 1 sheet of 8" x 10" ordinary white bond paper and a two speaker sound system. At each feeding, the following command was given repeatedly on tape: "Lanta, pick up the pencil and draw the tree." The last four years have produced no results. This year, for the first time, we added a tape recording of The Mormon Tabernacle Choir singing "Oh, Christmas Tree" and increased the protein content of her food by 50%. After only three days we observed Lanta suddenly seizing the pencil, forcing herself into an upright position and succeeding, though somewhat clumsily, in drawing the tree. That drawing is reproduced here in its actual size. This year marks our merriest Christmas since beginning our experiment. We want to share it with all our good friends. Merry Christmas!

CHRISTOPHER HEWAT

As the final hour drew near, there was a buzzing of merriment and activity at the North Pole....

Steve,
Happy
New Year!
Eugène

CREDITS

Drawing on title page by Brad Holland.
Typography by Leslie Cabarga.
Illuminated initials by Steven Guarnaccia.
Drawing on Artists page by Elliott Banfield.
Additional photography by Ed Spiro.
John Baeder: represented by O. K. Harris Gallery.
André Francois: pastel for friends and *Elle* magazine 1977.
Rockwell Kent: Philadelphia Museum of Art; given by Carl Zigrosser.
Paul Flora: printed by permission of Diogenese Verlag, A. G., Zurich.
Ilse Getz: represented by Monique Knowlton Gallery.
Alexander Walsh: courtesy Lerner-Heller Gallery.
Don Nice: courtesy Nancy Hoffman Gallery.
Ray Ciarrochi: courtesy Tibor Di Nagy Gallery.
Tomi Ungerer: printed by permission of Diogenese Verlag,
A. G., Zurich.
Art Spiegelman: courtesy Raw Books, Inc.
Edward Gorey: courtesy Edward Gorey.
Michael Knigen: published by Chiron Graphics, Ltd., NYC © 1978.
Gary Hallgren: created for Gorilla Graphics, San Francisco.
Allan Lewis: Philadelphia Museum of Art; given by Carl Zigrosser.
Randal Rupert: courtesy Randal Rupert.
Carol Anthony: represented by Monique Knowlton Gallery.
Hans P. Schaad: printed by permission of Diogenese Verlag,
A. G., Zurich.
Walt Kelly: © Walt Kelly, printed by permission of Selby Kelly,
executrix.
Jay Lynch: courtesy Krupp Comic Works, Inc.
Günter Grass: courtesy Lee Naiman.
Johnny Hart: B. C. by permission of Johnny Hart Enterprises, Inc.
Paul Cadmus: Philadelphia Museum of Art; given by Carl Zigrosser.
George Constant: courtesy Grace Borgenicht Gallery.
Alexander Calder: Philadelphia Museum of Art; given by
Carl Zigrosser.